Whispers of Grace

Carolina Christian Writers' Conference and

Southern California Christian Writers' Conference

Compiled by

Living Parables of Central Florida

Whispers of Grace

Stories • Devotions • Poems • Prayers

Volume 1

Copyright © 2020 Living Parables of Central Florida, Inc.

All rights reserved.

ISBN: 978-1-945975-50-9

Published by EA Books Publishing a division of
Living Parables of Central Florida, Inc. a 501c3
EABooksPublishing.com

Living Parables of Central Florida, Inc., of which EABooks Publishing is a division, offers publishing contests at Christian conferences to provide opportunities for unpublished authors to be discovered and earn publishing credits. We publish high quality, self-published books that bring glory and honor to God's Kingdom.

Can you hear it? Life often gets in the way of us hearing it — the roar of doubt, fear, and despair drown out the still small voice. But if we tune our ear to hear, it is there. Whispers of grace come to us when we lend our ear to the movements of God in our struggles, in our everyday lives, and in our hearts. May these stories, prayers, and poems create in you a desire to listen for the whispers of grace in your own life.

ACKNOWLEDGMENTS

We'd like to thank the directors of our conferences, Linda Gilden and Kathy Ide, for encouraging and equipping writers and speakers for the glory of the Kingdom of God. We wish to thank Cheri Cowell and her wonderful team at EABooks Publishing for giving us this opportunity. We thank our many friends and family for supporting us in our writing dreams. And most importantly, we want to thank our Lord and Savior Jesus Christ for His gifts—may this book bring You the honor and glory You deserve.

TABLE OF CONTENTS

Acknowledgments	iv

Carolina Christian Writers Conference

Story Power *Cathy Bannon Carden*	1
Whispers That Scream *Zylphia Ables*	7
Island in the Son *Trudy Brinling Goerk*	11
A Whisper From Heaven *Debbie Garrick*	13
Fingerprints *Val Halloran*	19
Precious G.E.M. (God's Extreme Makeover) *Michele Lawrence*	21
Grace on the Ground *L. A. Robbins*	27
God's Throne of Grace *Mona Selden*	31
One Voice, Under God *Linette Rainville*	33
The Season of Letting Go *Annette Wiley*	39

Southern California Christian Writers' Conference

You Are Loved   47
   Kim Caroline

How to View Your Life Like a Rubber Band   49
   G. Yvonne Mallory

Most Powerful Force   53
   D. H. Weinberg

Gracie   55
   Janene Zirges

Carolina Christian Writers Conference

Story Power

Cathy Bannon Carden

Ah, the ultimate expression of love. Is it as simple as compassionate forgiveness from the source who has the ultimate power over creation? In my own earthly life I have discovered the effects of grace in God's method of teaching us to think and learn. Having experienced his pure mercy in action fueled by his deep love to correct us rather than leave us in our messes has changed my life view forever. I have learned this not just through the Bible stories but through the life stories shared to me and lived by me. In reliving the past path there is truth which is tough to challenge. The vast power of storytelling belongs to the mightiest of warriors and the meekest of children. Through our true-life stories, we encourage others to think and learn by way of those precious lessons of grace God granted us. We each have our own testimony which ultimately belongs to God. It reminds me of the parable of the talents which is a good lesson on not burying the truth. As God has offered us Great Mercy by not taking the cup of wrath from Jesus, we owe our debt of gratitude by leveraging our saved life in ways so others might find their way to the kingdom of Light. Grace is the ultimate expression of love. The power of grace is found by our hero rescue through our God. Absolutely this is where giving joyful thanks to the Father kicks in and the hallelujah starts!

In the midst of God's deep love for us as his creation he fills those who are captured by that love with a longing for restoration and a discontent for settling in sin, driving us toward a purified desire for "more." For over two thousand years he has continually held open the narrow gateway to his ultimate daring rescue of us with the offer to reconnect our lost union with the God trinity. The gateway becomes narrower with time as the world chokes off the path by chasing God from the premise. Colossians 1:10 promises "so that you may live a life worthy of the Lord and please him in every way: bearing fruit in every good work, growing in the knowledge of God, being strengthened with all power according to his glorious might so that you may have great endurance and patience, and giving joyful thanks to the Father, who has qualified you to share in the inheritance of his holy people in the kingdom of light. For he has rescued us from the dominion of darkness and brought us into the kingdom of the Son he loves, in whom we have redemption, the forgiveness of sin."

As my own reminder I keep a scribbled reminder taped near my work desk that asks me what my message is: Will I judge and punish *or* will I help you think and learn? How do I love you? While this seems like common sense, the reality is that I am a messy single mom of five messy kids, most who got their start on this planet before I adopted them. All have been subject to above-average levels of childhood trauma and each has their overpacked Samsonite bag of wounds. We are collectively broken and often struggle with kind responses to each other because of those hard, past moments that continue to misshape our lives. Our redemption story is ongoing as is everyone's.

To be honest, even on the sweet occasion when I get out of bed filled to my hair follicles with the Holy Spirit, some wily child is getting out of their own bed with the subconscious plan of draining the Holy Spirit right back out of my toes. Our family motto has become "There's always one! combined with an eye roll. The burden of living in a fallen world is real, but most real for parents. By 6:15 in the morning I can lose my ability to believe I am living the worthy life or pleasing God because I am busy repelling the acronyms ODD, ADHD, PTSD, and RAD clothed in the skin of my youngest son.

Oppositional defiance disorder is maddening to contend with particularly before I have had even one cup of coffee. On my better days I cling to Ephesians 6:13 as my baseline survival promise. Evidently by putting on the full armor of God, when the day of evil comes, I will be able to stand my ground, and after I have done everything, to continue standing. I quietly mantra to myself in the first thirty minutes on those mornings, "Just stand, mama, just stand! Jesus! I'm seeing fiery darts here!" I question if ducking arrows qualifies as still standing.

What I often forget is that I do not have to physically fight. I should strive to endure with patience cloaked in love and armor up with the Word of God in order to squeeze out my own pittance of grace for the needs of my children. My son is not the day of evil, but he is excellent training to ready me when the day of evil takes over, and for sure it is near. This life is my story and there is a God path lit through the middle of the wild of it all that offers on the job training complete with a training manual and a Holy Spirit guide. As a bonus tool I seek the narratives of the stories of others I trust who have journeyed before me. Experience is valuable.

I often want to complain to God directly about the mess of life, but the conversation ends up looking much like historically embellished memories which spring up every Thanksgiving as my family laughingly reminisces about the dumb things we did as kids. I do not actually want to remind God that I, too, was/am his difficult child or that I have done dumb things. I muse in wonder if God has a note, or perhaps the entire King James version of the Bible taped to his window to remind him to help me think and learn rather than judge and punish.

Through God's years of patient correcting combined with endless natural consequences my greatest regrets lie in the years I ran from him, but never once in the years I have chosen to walk holding his hand. Deep in my heart I understand the power of his rescue from the dominion of darkness. In my long-ago life, not only did I walk in the valley of the shadow of death, I operated as a tour guide. Through epic sin-stacked obstacles I bumbled over, under, and through, I know for sure there is the mercy of teaching grace-filled hope for others. For it turns out that in every wrong turn there is a right opportunity to redeem a mistake. This does not alleviate the concept of consequences as they still apply but this is where the story turns toward true restoration. Isaiah 9:2 surprises me by its content. "The people who walked in darkness have seen a great light; those who dwelt in the land of the shadow of death upon them a light has shined." The God-sized light bulb for sure shines bright.

Much truth lies in the old adage, "If he can save me, he can save anybody." Perhaps the heart of the matter is in the "anybody." It's the same person as the "whosoever" in John 3:16. God transcends the lamenting depths of too far down and too wide open, too much or too little. There is nowhere to run from him. Just see Jonah's story about that whale belly hiding spot. Not being in synergy with God's big dreams through us gets a little fishy. I, too, ran from God and hid everywhere *but* in the fish. My life seems to back up many Bible stories I have noticed.

God will pursue us intentionally until we are swept up in his love or he is finally convinced of our dramatic "no" and stops asking. In my story, no matter how far I ran, he was already there as he never let go of me. I physically felt his promise of commitment in my soul. I may add here that the worst of my life choices came after asking Jesus into my heart. God honored my desire to want to love him even when I struggled to love myself. Just because no one teaches spiritual warfare as a real thing will not diminish its reality.

The end game to our rescue lands us in the kingdom of Light, the kingdom of his Son. We become caught up in his loving embrace through his son Jesus as he shines his love through what we did *not* receive because of his mercy protection and by the grace which gave us humility to learn. With these grace-filled experiences packed personal tales we are commissioned and armed to stand outside the very gates of hell and offer our true stories of rescue to those who are still blinking their way through darkness.

Even though we may not witness the effects of our stories, we are always called to plant the seeds for those with ready ears. Soul growth is not our burden unless it's our own soul. The greatest thing Jesus will ever do for us, he has already done and continues to do. I know he diminished my day of judgment the day I ran to him seeking rescue from myself and the world. Though it was never his will, God absolutely allowed the death of my six-year-old at the hands of cancer twelve years ago. Only then could I truly understand the concepts of rescue, eternity, loving deeply, not fearing death, and redeeming loss through adoption. I am aware of where she is which is in my heart-hope future reunion.

This is not remotely the story I would have written for myself because it has sad parts and hard parts and loads of stuff I would have liked to avoid. Yet I watch in amazement as my life is filled with unexpected God encounters directing my life toward redemption. The story I walk and tell can become the tie between life and hope for others even with the many sad and bad parts.

As we seek the life abundant we ought to press in to developing the ability to share what is our gift. Every Christian has a story. Would we punish our friends and neighbors by not sharing our life stories or will we strive through our own gift of grace to love and help them learn? Consider the power of simply telling your story, even the sad and bad parts for in the kingdom of God, there will be the very happy ending.

Cathy Carden is a word-gardener sowing life stories of love, humor, and honesty. Rooted in Jesus, she vocalizes platforms of adoption, child trauma, and special needs. For fun she plows life wide open via flash RV trips with her family; as an entrepreneur she runs her own brick and mortar business set in a 100-year-old small-town grocery store.

Whispers That Scream

Zylphia Ables

The daughter of a slave heard a whisper. She believed the angel who stood beside her told her to paint or die. She chose to paint. Her name was Minnie Evans. She painted visions from God and is today one of the best known and sought after primitive visionary artists who has ever lived. She listened.

As a child I was blessed to have known Minnie Evans. She would hum "Jesus loves me" while she shared her color crayons and paper at her kitchen table with me. She shared her talent and love of the Lord with me. Minnie told me she thought God's favorite color must have been green because of all of the beautiful trees and plants and I should remember this whenever I chose green. Minnie's stories of Noah and his ark, Sampson and the Lion, David and the Giant, the angel that stood beside her, were whispers of grace she so tenderly shared with me as a child that still reverberate to my soul. Minnie told me that if God should choose to speak to me that I must listen.

I am blessed by Minnie's art works I am able to see every day. By God's grace and her willingness to listen she painted Christ on the cross at Golgotha. What is it trying to say? What is the meaning here? Christ died on the cross for me. By his grace he died for me. Every day I see another of Minnie's paintings of Jesus smiling with arms open wide as he leaves the tomb. Jesus lives! Another painting of a wheel with seven stars and seven balls encircled between two angelic beings shows each holding azure blue foliage. An emerald green beast with a scroll in its mouth is on the left with three large eyes and a wing that is circular with nine eyes in the wing. There is a horseshoe of twenty-two eyes with a burgeoning tree and its root ball between a white-winged horse-like creature with three eyes. On the ground there are three small trees and three white birds larger than the trees. I do not understand these things now. My faith is in Jesus. One day I know I will live with him forever in paradise. Jesus loves me.

Whispers of grace resound! Do you take the time to hear? How many times has God's grace whispered to each of us?

God's grace whispers when I see Minnie Evans' artwork, in the smile of an infant, in the flutter of butterfly wings, and in the whisper of a rainbow after a storm. What and when do you hear it? Are we listening intently enough? Is our attention undivided?

Know the LORD! Share your blessings, skills, time, and talents. Teach a child the Bible stories you know. Make God's heart rejoice when he thinks of you. God can send whispers of grace to your conscience because he is omnipresent, omniscient, and omnipotent. He has a perfect plan for you. He has a special assignment just for you. You are the only one of you he has created. He whispers grace to your conscience not because he doesn't want you to enjoy life, but because he wants you to enjoy the best life. God loves you. Jesus loves you. God will use your experiences to reveal himself to you and to do something good not only in your life but in the lives of others. God will supply all of your needs because of your relationship with Christ Jesus. God gives his children the best blessings and God knows the desires of our hearts. Romans 10:17 teaches that faith comes from hearing. Hearing is from the grace of God. God's grace is a gift from our heavenly father through his son Christ Jesus. Jesus is all we truly need.

When God whispers, know that it is a scream of his grace that he loves you.

Zylphia Ables is a Child of God, a Christian, a minister's wife, and a mother. She is a graduate of Campbell University. A sinner saved by God's grace, Zylphia wants to be a blessing to others and to make God's heart rejoice when he thinks of her. Zylphia wants to always hear God's whispers and respond in a way that pleases him.

Whispers

Island in the Son

Trudy Brinling Goerk

Dark sleep
Earth awakens
Gulls herald–
colors of the dawn.
Sun rises over the ocean
Waves crash and roar.

Genesis–
two lovers,
One flesh united.
Seasons passing
Somnolence.

Deception–
Sin, separation, soil.
Heaven crying–
tears of dew.
Nightfall
darkness hovers.
Hope dying.
What is man–
of earth–
to do?

✦

Heaven answers.
Tides of mercy–
Crest and fall.
Conception
Labor
A Son–
The Peace Child
Born.
His life — love eternal
Incarnate.
His destiny — death.
Embracing a cross

✦

All is lost?
No…
Wait.
Easter Morn.
Resuscitation
Resurrection
Redemption
Hope–
Restored.
Refreshed
Reborn
Rejoice!
Co-laborers — God and Man
Eden again.

Trudy Brinling Goerk, a Registered Nurse, B. S. N., is published in the American Journal of Nursing. A cancer survivor, Trudy shared her story in Cancer Overcomers: Gold Refined by Fire, the Thirteen P's, accompanied by the Booklet Guide for the Cancer Patient During Active Treatment and the Leaders Guide, the Thirteen R's.

A Whisper from Heaven

Debbie Garrick

He was my spiritual mentor, wise counselor, and, despite the fifty-plus-years between our birthdays, one of my dearest friends. Those closest to him called him Preach, a moniker most lovingly expressed by his grandchildren.

It was early November when he called to remind me of a promise made years ago to deliver his eulogy when the time came. As he shared the oncologist's bleak prognosis, I understood the time was coming soon. A visit followed, during which he produced a small spiral notebook, ripped out a blank page, and thrust it into my hand.

"These are the things you need to know."

His authoritative edict sent me fumbling through my purse for a pen while he flipped another page in the notebook. I could see five numbered items penned in shaky cursive. He read them aloud and quickly acknowledged the words should be familiar. It was true. The list included maxims he had shared with me on numerous occasions.

1. *If you work and study consistently, you will achieve success.*
2. *If you help others, it will come back to you, and you will live a happy life.*
3. *Worry and unresolved concern are no good and will profit nothing.*
4. *The positive life is 100% better than the negative life.*
5. *Trust in the Lord God and He will direct thy paths. You must believe in yourself, because God made you!*

I found it interesting that he had distilled a lifetime of wisdom into five simple points. I visited several more times between Thanksgiving and Christmas, hoping with each trip that the list would grow. Those five truths seemed less than sufficient to guide me in the days ahead.

During one visit, he motioned me into his study, signaling the conversation would be weighty. He leaned forward and whispered, "Talk to me about spiritual things." The request caught me off guard. After all, he was the one with the seminary degree.

Before me sat the man who taught me to memorize scripture when I was ten years old. Preach was convinced that knowing scripture eclipsed solving mysteries with Scooby Doo and the gang. As a result, I'd spent more than a few Saturday mornings standing at attention as Preach directed a group of cartoon-deprived children to "draw swords and charge" with the rigor of a Camp Lejeune master sergeant. (For those unfamiliar with a Bible sword drill, a conversation with any Sunday School teacher in the rural South will provide a quick education.)

His serious request to discuss spiritual things brought to my mind the call I'd received just before my freshman year of college. The voice on the phone was sweeter than my grandmother's banana pudding. "Preach would like to speak to you before you leave town," his wife summoned. This was not a request. I arrived to find him seated in the Boston rocker, hands folded. His gaze was fixed toward the big bay window in his den, allowing him to view the ducks gathering on the pond.

After a most dramatic pause, he proceeded to recite a litany of potential temptations I might face as a college student. While scholarly failure could be overcome, he cautioned, a failure of character might not afford the same grace. There would be few opportunities to improve a grade regarding my reputation. He gave tips on how to study and offered advice on choosing the *right* friends, asserting that college friends would be friends for life. No topic—from men to gin—was off limits. His frankness both terrified and pleased me. I suddenly felt incredibly grown up.

I was aware Preach had once lived in my college town, so I was not surprised when he concluded the conversation by providing a list of friends and family who lived within blocks of campus. I contacted them all, and through the years they provided a great deal of comfort and plenty of home-cooked meals.

On my twenty-first birthday, I received a letter announcing gifts of stock had been purchased to celebrate that milestone. Money from Preach never came without advice. The letter read, "This gift is tithe money to the Lord, so you will know the care with which it is to be used...the money will be available for your use whenever you call for it, but I had thought that it might be used in your postgraduate studies." A generous gift and a not so subtle suggestion paved the way for me to continue my education. Preach was there when I received my master's degree and could hardly contain his joy years later when he learned I was pursuing a doctorate.

His support for me was always timely. When I was asked to speak at the funeral of a mutual friend, I called Preach in a panic. "I've been asked to do something that I don't think I have the strength to do." He calmed me quickly by replying, "You *can* do it. You *will* do it, and I will help you." At the service he ushered me to the seat beside him. As I stood to speak, he whispered, "You *can* do it. I'll be praying for you," and as I returned to my seat, he grabbed my hand and said, "That's my girl."

It was that familial bond we shared that found me at a pulpit again, this time to deliver the eulogy for his beloved bride of sixty-six years. Preach was doubly blessed to have been married to two beautiful women in his lifetime.

Between the loss of his first wife and finding his second love, he sent me a letter while on a family vacation in Europe. The first line read, "I certainly need a woman to look after me! I failed to put stamps on a postcard I sent you from Ireland." That postcard *had* arrived, even without the stamp, and in it he teased that he was looking for a "redheaded lassie" to bring home with him. A few days later, another card arrived, this one postmarked from Scotland. It read, "I proposed to a redhead and told her I owned a castle, but she was already married. That's my luck!"

The avalanche of memories came to a sudden halt as Preach cleared his throat, bringing me back to the reality of the cold December day. The time had come for Preach to receive something from me.

I had witnessed a life that exemplified far more than those five simple truths scrawled in a notebook a few weeks prior. I was humbled by his invitation to talk about spiritual things and hoped his wisdom through the years would provide what I needed to render comfort in this moment.

"What kind of spiritual things do you want to talk about?" I asked.

"Nobody likes to talk about death. Are you afraid to talk about it?"

"No, sir."

"Well, neither am I. Let's talk about it. Tell me what you think is going to happen. How do you think it's gonna go?"

The cancer had affected his stomach, and he mentioned the pain was constant. I thought back to those Bible drills and tried to remember something relevant.

"Well, Preach, I believe it's biblical that one of the jobs God gave the angels was to escort us into heaven. I think he will send an angel for you, and I feel sure it won't hurt a bit."

He smiled and said, "I like the sound of that!"

I came by several more times in the weeks to follow, but on the day before New Year's Eve, I sensed this would be my last visit. He was bedridden now and weaker, but he was still in good spirits. As I approached the bedside, he whispered, "They're beginning to get concerned."

"Yes, sir, I know."

"Heaven . . . tell me again, how do you think it's gonna go?"

I reminded him of our previous conversation and assured him the very best angel would surely be sent as his traveling companion. He lifted his head from the pillow, straining to see something just over my shoulder.

I turned around thinking someone had joined us in the room, but no one had entered.

"What do you see?" I asked.

"I think he's here," he whispered, "look at that light."

I turned again but saw no one. The only light in the room came from a lamp on the bedside table.

A few days later, I stood before a gathering of family and friends to fulfill my promise to Preach. The bulk of my remarks centered on the words scrawled before me on a simple piece of notebook paper.

As I returned to my seat, a whisper from heaven gently fell in my ear.

"That's my girl."

Debbie Garrick is a Development Officer at her alma mater, Winthrop University, where she earned both a B.A. in Journalism and M.Ed. in Counseling. She also holds an Ed.D. from Nova Southeastern University. Her superpowers include a dry wit and the ability to consume Krispy Kreme donuts without guilt.

Fingerprints

Val Halloran

His fingerprints are on my life;
I've come to know and see;
His hands are always first to hold
Each thing that touches me.
Nothing will escape His grasp;
He takes and shapes for good
Even what seems hard and wrong
And things misunderstood.

Fingerprints of mercy,
Fingerprints of grace,
Reaching, touching, showing me
Reflections of His face.
Fingerprints, so gentle,
Forever left their mark
The day He came and touched my life
And healed my broken heart.

Sometimes it seems that random things
Just come to us by chance,
That there's no rhyme or reason
And it's all just circumstance.
But God is there behind the scenes,
I often miss the hints.
I'm learning as the days go by
To see His fingerprints.

Fingerprints of mercy,
Fingerprints of grace,
Reaching, touching, showing me
Reflections of His face.
Fingerprints so gentle,
Forever they will stay,
To show that I am not my own,
He's the potter, I'm the clay.
Come, Jesus, now and touch my life.
Your fingerprints will stay.

Val Halloran is a wife, mother, grandmother, and singer/songwriter. Her songs have been featured on radio stations across the globe. She writes from her heart of her personal walk with God, in hopes of encouraging others who can relate to the sentiments expressed through her writing.

Precious G.E.M.
(God's Extreme Makeover)

Michele Lawrence

I'm not a big fan of using acronyms, but this one, "Precious G.E.M." just feels good. When I was young, it was instilled in me that what happened in our home stayed there. So I became, what I thought, was a very private person, when in reality, I was just afraid. All of us have experienced loss, pain, fear, disappointment, and hurt, which often turns into anger, depression, guilt, and the list goes on.

This is my story—I was a mess. You can imagine my surprise when I started the study of the New Testament and realized how much I had been lied to and how much I hadn't been told. I experienced feelings similar to a person grieving. The shock and anger of accepting that the majority of my life as I knew it, was not based in biblical truth. This led to feelings of loneliness and a fear of how I would survive in a whole new way of life. I never knew I could have a personal relationship with Jesus, so as I was urged to start stepping out and sharing my story with others, I realized He'd been there all along. With His love, I was experiencing for the first time what being "born again" really meant. Today, I'm going through the stages of my recovery, which are filled with blessings, both big and small.

A big blessing occurred the day I was re-baptized. I wanted it to be a private party with just my immediate family and a few close friends. Then my pastor and my husband explained to me why it would be pleasing to God to be baptized in public. They both said it might help others to feel the joy and freedom I was experiencing. I agreed and was told that there were usually twenty to thirty people each time they held a baptism. I was comforted by the thought of being able to hide among others who would be baptized that day, too. But God had other plans.

That morning I was in a huge church, full of strangers, with my image on the big screen as I stood in a bathtub. I focused on my husband, son, and my pastor, Ted Stone, who were all by my side. Yes, I was the only one who showed up that morning to be baptized. Be careful what you pray for . . . I got my private baptism.

I thought I was doing pretty well at this point in my life, until I arrived in the big state of Texas for a weeklong wellness retreat. You see, another big mess followed me there in the form of the thoughts that had been put into my mind by some of my friends and extended family. They feared that I would be brainwashed, or worse yet, I was going to join a cult and I would never be seen again. Since I had never been to any type of retreat before, Satan was having a lot of fun with me in the weeks before I arrived. I spent the first night in tears, mostly wondering how I would survive a week with women I didn't know, being out in the middle of nowhere with no television, lamenting over how bored and lonely I would be.

The next morning, as I walked downstairs into the "unknown," I heard a voice, "Hey, Michele! Come on now, let's go for a walk." I immediately looked down at the new bright, white tennis shoes I had bought for just such an occasion and accepted the invitation. So, with Carole Lewis by my side, who has since, as Jesus would have it, become my "Spiritual Momma," we walked and talked and kept on walking. She kept saying how grateful she was for the nice weather that day in Texas, but all this girl from California could think about was how humid it was and just how much farther we were going to walk. I knew how far we had already come, which meant we were going to have to walk that far back...then we came upon a large building—a concert hall. Carole started to tell me about it and how she wished she could show me the inside but the doors were always locked. Guess what? Not that day—and they even had the air conditioning on. It felt so good to be in the cool air and also in such a beautiful grand hall. Since I was a little girl, I had always dreamed of singing in a grand hall like this one. You see, singing in front of large crowds was one of the things in my life that didn't scare me. So there we were, just Carole and I, when I heard a still, small voice say, "Go up on stage." With a little nudge from Carole, I climbed the stairs to the stage and Carole took a seat in the middle of the hall. As I stood there on the stage dreaming, Carole asked if I would sing one of my songs. So, with God as my accompanist, I opened my mouth and filled the beautiful room.

While at Round Top Retreat in Texas that week, I was blessed with so much love and a feeling of security, that I finally understood what the song "Amazing Grace" is all about. I was called "Precious" so many times that week that I really started to believe I was. The way the word precious made me feel was a feeling I hadn't associated with myself.

When I got home and was sitting at my piano, God reminded me of how Precious we *all* are to Him. I was already spending daily time in the Word, but now, for some reason, His Word, His love and His sacrifice for me took on a whole new meaning. I've since learned to wait on God and when there is absolutely no question or confusion, that's when I know it's Him. So He put on my heart these words, which originally came in the form of a love letter, simply addressed to:

My Precious One,

You're perfect in every way, that's all I'm gonna say. I feel I belong here, how 'bout you? So If you would stay for a while, I sure do miss that smile, because it feels like sunshine keepin' the clouds away. It's gonna be a good day, Precious. It's as simple as holding you here in my arms, it's a good day. Because I found the place in your heart that needed some extra attention, My Precious One.

I knew it wouldn't take me long to write you this simple love song. Just know it's the truth. So if you could stay for a while, because you know I sure do love that smile. Would you be my sunshine, forever and always? It's gonna be a good day, Precious. Simple love is gonna carry us through to the next day, you just wait and see. Because the love I feel in my heart, when I look in your eyes, is worth so much more than any amount of money could ever buy. You see I found that place in your heart that needs some extra attention, My Precious One.........Jesus

"But let your adorning be the hidden person of the heart, with the imperishable beauty of a gentle and quiet spirit, which in God's sight is very Precious" (1 Peter 3:4 ESV).

With the receipt of this love letter, I've experienced how God sometimes uses people who love you to invite you into His presence with something as simple as a word. "Precious" was the word I kept hearing and I finally received the gift of His Precious love, which has transformed me from the inside out. The love letter seemed to already have a rhyme and rhythm to it and became one of the first songs I wrote, simply entitled, "Precious."

Since the writing of "Precious," Jesus has put on my heart many songs which have inspired, healed, and encouraged not only myself but others. My latest surprise blessing came to me when I finally realized how important memorizing scripture would be. So my recent music projects have been with the passion of helping to memorize scriptures through music. It has been amazing to be able to call up scripture that is now forever on my heart...and sing it!

"How precious to me are Your thoughts, God! How vast is the sum of them! Were I to count them, they would outnumber the grains of sand...when I awake, I am still with You" (Psalm 139:17-18 NIV).

Michele Lawrence, singer and songwriter, loves performing live, telling the story behind her songs, and weaving together the stories of a lifetime. A vocal coach, worship leader, inspirational speaker, blessed wife, and mother, Michele's music is streaming on YouTube, Apple Music, Spotify, Google Play, Pandora, and Amazon. Contact her at michele-lawrence@att.net or Facebook@michelelawrencemusic.

Whispers of Grace

Grace on the Ground

L. A. Robbins

His heart beat wildly as he moved toward the babbling brook. His ruddy face conveyed the intensity of the task looming before him. A mixture of determination, excitement, and fear were expressed in his dark brown eyes. His older brother accused him of showing up because he was a naughty and prideful young lad and the king claimed the task was too daunting for this young shepherd boy. He was ill-equipped to face a giant of great stature who was a man of war from his youth. Impossible odds, they all claimed, but he knew better. While watching his father's sheep he had killed a lion and a bear with supernatural strength provided by his God. As he leaned down to pick up five smooth stones he wondered why all the others were allowing this uncircumcised Philistine to mock God. He would not allow such disgusting behavior from this vile giant. Someone had to quiet his constant threats and insulting slander of the one and only true God of Israel. Divine assistance was available to anyone who chose to believe and he chose to believe. Five stones were now safely secured in the young lad's scrip and he donned his sling across his shoulder. He had become very skilled with his sling while daily serving on the Judean hillside. He would stand against this giant with what he knew would work. To step into the armor offered by the king would only prove to weigh him down so his protection would be divinely provided. As the giant drew near he looked down upon his opponent with a slur of mockery. His loud curses and threats rang in the youth's ears but a strong reply burst forth from the mouth of the young Judean boy. The giant depended on his sword, spear, and shield but this youngster was coming in the name of the Lord of Hosts, the God of Israel. This battle belonged to God. Skilled hands selected a stone from the scrip and placed it in his sling. Lean muscles and living faith ran to meet the giant as the sling released the swirling smooth rock through the air. The stone accelerated and smote the Philistine sinking solidly into his forehead. He fell face first; victory was attained because one little Hebrew boy relied on his God for divine assistance. Five smooth stones from the brook bed and the assistance of his Savior was the method that worked four thousand years ago.

She was clothed in shame and nothing more as her accusers drug her sinful body before the Savior. The critiquing clutch of religious men had caught her in the very act of adultery. She was guilty but the man she had fornicated with had been left behind. As she stood in the middle of the crowd, humiliation filled her whole body. Heat rose to her face as she perceived the judgment upon the faces of the men who had brought her to Jesus. They addressed him as master and explained that she was taken in the very act of adultery. She could not deny these claims because they were true. They wanted to stone her according to the Law of Moses but they probed Jesus as to what he would recommend. Their demeaning accusations did not appear to influence this man Jesus but he was a Jew so surely he would abide by the law. Her fate was in his hands. What he did next sealed her future. He simply stooped down and wrote on the ground with his finger as if he did not hear her accusers at all. More questions came with still no answers. Jesus lifted himself up and commanded that if any of her faultfinding foes were without sin they were to cast the first stone. He again stooped down and wrote on the ground. What was this man named Jesus writing? She was bewildered and somewhat confused. To her amazement the oldest man who had assisted in bringing her to the Savior left, followed by the remaining men. She stood naked before Jesus, wide eyed and helpless. He lifted himself up from the ground. Her Gentile eyes met his Jewish eyes and she felt peace. As he quietly inquired of her accuser's whereabouts and if she had been condemned, she was astounded. No man was left to condemn her and neither did her Lord. He simply stated for her to go and sin no more. She knew she did not deserve this gift from Jesus but she felt an overpowering satisfaction in her soul that no other man would ever fill. This Jesus was gracious and kind and had assisted her in her time of need. As she walked away she knew that she was free from the guilt of sin and shame. Whatever he wrote on the ground was a mystery but it worked two thousand years ago.

    She was young and struggling to make sense of the pain she felt from her parents' troubled marriage. Her dad's affair with her mom's friend had left her mom in a dreadful state. Weight loss, mental stress, and emotional abuse had taken a toll on her mom's body and soul. Sometimes anger engulfed her teenage body as she witnessed the devastating effects of indulging in sin without regard to God or family. She had to come to terms with the fact that this behavior belonged to her parents and she must choose to cope as best she could under the circumstances. In the midst of the turmoil she knew she needed a Savior. She had just turned sixteen and wanted a relationship with Jesus. As she lay in bed each night her cries of repentance and desperation were heard by the heavenly Father. Her mother took her to church and she later attended with her boyfriend. Young and ignorant she floundered through her junior and senior year of high school and married five months after graduation. Her first baby girl arrived nineteen months later followed by another baby girl twenty-one months thereafter. While still attending church during her second pregnancy she began to wonder if she had truly been born again. The struggle was real but her complete surrender to her Savior settled her troubled heart. She knew Jesus had left heaven and came to earth to dwell among men. He faced a cruel scourging and shed his blood on the cross that was placed into the hardened ground on the hillside of Golgotha. His mutilated body was buried in a borrowed tomb to arise again victorious over death, hell, and the grave. Complete peace took abode as she accepted his unmerited divine favor. God regenerated her heart and she was a new creature. Thirty years later his assistance still remains. Battle scars left by verbal abuse, church abuse, and tough ministry have never been able to erase his grace that is sufficient for all who believe both past and present.

LA. Robbins is an aspiring author who feels called to write with a purpose to encourage women and children. She lives in rural Tennessee with her husband. She is a mother of three adult children and Nana to two sweet girls.

God's Throne of Grace

Mona Selden

"Let us then with confidence draw near to the throne of grace, that we may receive mercy and find grace to help in time of need."
~ Hebrews 4:16 (ESV)

How are we able to approach God's throne of grace? How is it that we cannot just approach but draw near with confidence? And what do we receive at His throne of grace?

In Hebrews, we read it is because of Jesus, our great high priest, that we can approach God's throne. Jesus, who passed through the heavens and is sitting at the right hand of God. Jesus, who was tempted in all things as we are, but was without sin. Jesus, who sympathizes with our weaknesses. He gives us our confidence. We just need to look to Jesus, and we will have the confidence we need to draw near to God's throne.

What temptations are you facing? What do you struggle with? What threatens to undo you? Jesus has felt the same. He has faced those temptations and struggles. But we know that Jesus did not sin; He found a way out of the temptation.

Won't He then show you the way out? Where are you feeling weak? What makes you feel as if you just can't go on, as if you just can't stand anymore? Remember that Jesus sympathizes with your weaknesses. He knows, He understands, He has walked through it all.

We all have times of need, and when we draw near to the throne of grace, we will receive mercy and find grace to help.

What need do you have for God's mercy? Have you fallen into sin? Have you messed up? Have you mistreated someone? Have you lost your way? Draw near to His throne and you will receive mercy. Or perhaps you are tired of walking the path God has set you on – tired of the struggles, tired of the pain. Maybe you feel weak without any strength to continue enduring the storm. Maybe this season of life has left you dry, and you have nothing left to give. Come to the throne of grace, with confidence, and you will find grace to help you to continue, to endure, to be strong, to give. You will find grace to help you no matter what today holds, or what tomorrow will bring.

Take time right now to draw near to God's throne. Jesus is there waiting to give you all the mercy and all the grace that you need. You only need to seek it and receive it.

Mona Selden writes daily devotions for her church in south-central Virginia. She has taught Bible studies for nearly twenty years and has written devotions for other ministries. She and her husband, Tyler, are enjoying their nearly empty nest with a son in college and a married daughter.

One Voice, Under God

Linette Rainville

I hear Him whispering.
"I see you daughter.
I see all you've been through and how far you've come.
It's time.
It's time for you step into all that I've prepared for you."
Sisters, do we not hear His call?
Do we not feel His Spirit stirring in us to raise our voices?
The chaos, catastrophe, hurt, and pain we are seeing in our world truly breaks the Father's heart just as it breaks ours.
Women are His grace carriers—as His daughters we have been uniquely equipped.
We are nurturers, we are caregivers, we are lovers of people.
In this hour, the Lord has a strategic plan to use us to pour out His unfailing love across our land, across denominations, across cultures, and across generations.
God is calling out the gifts He has placed inside of you and me,
to help heal and defend our land.
This is our Esther Calling.
He is calling us to rise up, together, as one voice . . . under God.
The Lord desires His Holy Spirit to shine ever brighter in this growing darkness,
but He needs earthen vessels to shine through.
We are such vessels.
We are His torchbearers.
He is uniting us to shine.

In the days of Esther, the king's decree gave God's people authority to assemble, unite, and defend their lives (Esther 8:11).
I can hear God's word echoing in my heart for us today,
"Go forth, I am sending you in my strength,
in my power, and with my authority.
Here, I have written the royal decree.
Go!
Today I give you the authority to unite,
gather, and to defend your lives and your nation."
Will we be brave?
Or will we stay silent?

In the day of Charles Finney, the Lord blew a holy fire into the hearts of many sons and daughters. Yes, even His daughters. In that day, the law of the land limited the voices of women,
but they became brave and spoke out despite the opposition . . . as one voice.
Today, there is no law holding us back.
Sisters, where are our virtuous voices?
This is our Esther Calling.
As we pray, fast, and gather as one voice, we-together, can send out a *holy roar* across this nation and around the world.
I can hear the Father reassuring our hearts,
"I will be with you, just as I was with Esther.
I am filling you with my power and my presence to stand up as a voice to your generation."
The Lord continues . . .
"Daughters,
this is your set time.
There has never been a better time in recent history than now for you to gather and unite as *one* in heart and purpose.
As you cry out for the righteous roots of America to regain her strength, I will redeem you.

As you walk out my love, pouring good works upon the land, you shall bring glory to my name.
As you join together as one voice, you will resound one powerful, mama-bear roar.
A virtuous roar.
One that will prevail against the darkness that has invaded your land.
America will once again be called the land of the free and the home of the brave.
Daughters, you no longer need to wait for a movement,
You ARE the movement!
You shall be a movement that will stand strong against the evils of this world.
You are my mighty army, my brides in boots!
Go forth!
For I am sending you."

Love,
Your Father, God

"From women it was birthed,
by women it became twisted,
and through God's Women rising
it can become righteous." —Linette Rainville

Women on Mountains
Linette Rainville, journal entry January 17, 2020

I woke up with an incredible dream this morning.
In my dream, I saw that mountains were rising up all over our country and women leaders were standing on top of those mountains. They were calling out to the Lord and

beckoning their sisters to join them on that mountain. Big ones and little ones were sprouting up everywhere!
I inquired of the Lord and He said, *"PRAY!"*
"Pray for these mighty mountains to rise up; Daughters who will be my ambassadors,
who will intercede on that mountain for their country and their people.
For I am releasing an Esther Calling. I am raising up leaders over states, over cities, over territories, over ministries, and industries, who shall be my foot soldiers to take the land!
My Brides in Boots!
Fast and pray. Train and take arms for the Lord your God has spoken this decree!
Watch and see the mighty right hand of your Father move on your behalf!
The landscape of your nation is about to change!"
"And who knows but that you have come to your royal position for such a time as this?"
(Esther 4:14)

My Dear Sister,
You have a niche, an influence, a territory that is assigned to you.
Know what you carry.
No one else can reach your world the way you can.
Go ahead . . . stand on your mountain,
lift high your sword,
and take the ground that the Father has given you.

Love, Linette
Daughters United
Visionary/Founder

God's Strategic Plan to Take the Land:

- Gather together in my name, all of you in one place (Nehemiah 8:1).
- Pray for the anointing of my love and presence to come upon you (Psalm 36:10).
- Pour this love and presence everywhere your foot touches (Deuteronomy. 11:24).
- Develop and deploy the plans I am giving you to take back lost territory (Joshua 1:6-7).
- Raise up a virtuous voice in government, media, and education (Proverbs 31:8).
- Heal my church, bring love, respect, and honor to each part of my body (1 Corinthians 12 &13).

"I pray that they will all be one, just as you and I are one–as you are in me, Father, and I am in you. And may they be in us so that the world will believe you sent me" (John 17:21 NLT).

Linette Rainville is a chaplain, U.S. Navy veteran and sister-friend to all who know her. She serves as CEO, visionary and national voice of Christian women at Daughters United. You'll love her warm, authentic, gutsy spirit inspiring you to "Do what you can, right where you are, with what you have." Website: www.DaughtersUnited.org Email: linette@daughtersunited.org.

The Season of Letting Go

Annette Wiley

Most of my cherished childhood memories involve the Christmases shared with my family. Every year my father would plow through the front door wrestling to pull a gigantic evergreen tree into the house. The crisp scent wafted throughout with a fresh and clean fragrance. A kaleidoscope of ornaments dressed the tree while the beloved angel perched at the top. With the tree-trimming complete, we gathered outside to admire our handiwork through the large picture window. Next, we piled in the car and drove throughout our neighborhood enjoying all the vibrant decorations, while listening to carols on the radio. The Christmas season was always magical. One day the neighborhood looked normal and then poof! a menagerie of color erupted everywhere.

Those precious memories inspired me to create the wonder of the season for my family. Each year, I endeavored to bring a bit of magic to our home. The yard would be strung with thousands of lights. On the front porch, five trees stood tall, decked with streams of red ribbon, bows, and twinkling lights.

Every year, bin upon bin of decorations and enough trees for every room would be scattered throughout. I made countless trips up and down the stairs and spent endless hours decorating each room *just so*. I loved every minute of it!

Except for this past year.

Anxiety had simmered in me for weeks. The volcano of apprehension erupted the Friday morning after

Thanksgiving, leaving me bewildered. The usual excitement to decorate fizzled out of me while my energy level dropped like the barometric pressure of an incoming weather front. As much as I had wanted our family time to be less stressful and more relaxed, I couldn't imagine how that would happen. I was at my wit's end thinking about several church-related commitments written in big bold letters on my calendar. Decorating the house for Christmas was just the first of many tasks that loomed on the horizon like a gathering storm. A mental checklist of upcoming duties whizzed around in my head. I knew there would scarcely be time to breathe until sometime in March. As I imagined a quarter of my year slipping through my fingers like sand, my heart raced in response.

Depressed and weary, I decided to severely streamline our decorations for Christmas. I fretted that everyone would be disappointed and I imagined glum faces and comments about the absence of so many of the treasured trees. The family room tree would have to do. I decorated without much enthusiasm and I knew this Christmas would surely be different.

Soon the family members arrived and settled in. Laughter and conversation ensued like always. Card games were played and Play-Doh bakery treats covered the kitchen table. Several days passed and no one mentioned the missing trees. I smiled as I wondered, had I been the only one excited about the extra trees after all? Joy and delight shone on every face. Everyone was relaxed and happy. Except for me. I was caught in a battle to stay in the moment and enjoy the children laughing, babies giggling, and watching my grown sons and husband compete in various silly games. Five generations had gathered here for a short time, and I had been anxious and pre-occupied with all the other "stuff" vying for my attention. Right then the scripture passage Luke 10:38-42 flitted across my thoughts. In the scripture, Jesus pointed out to Martha that she was anxious about many things while her sister, Mary, had chosen the better part. She chose to live in the moment at the feet of Jesus. The message of the scripture was not lost on me.

Feeding so many guests had required that I make countless trips to the grocery store. One afternoon I struggled through the door, my hands laden with bags. Noticing a stunning fresh floral arrangement on the kitchen island, I breathed in the evergreen scent. My heart took a leap as I read the lovely message my college-freshman granddaughter had written to me. She thanked me for the countless ways I worked so hard to make Christmas special for everyone. Grateful tears spilled over. Her thoughtfulness was a balm to my soul. Through her lovely gift and precious message, God winked at me, allowing me to understand that He had encouraged me to focus less on the trimmings and more on the essence of our family celebration. During the few remaining days of the visit I focused on the joy that surrounded me. But, much too quickly, the time came for heartfelt goodbyes and lots of hugs.

With my husband back at work, I had the house to myself. Anxiety raised its ugly head yet again while chaos stirred in my soul. The time came for me to tend to all the details as director of the upcoming women's retreat and assume the usual role as Girl Friday for the men's retreat. My mind raced as I wondered when I would have time to finally take down our Christmas decorations. I realized, with a deflated spirit, that perhaps sometime in March our home might get back to normal. My mind reeled with the prospect.

January and February flew by in a flurry of activity for the retreats. As always, God had led the way, and the retreats were a great success. March arrived with a shroud of vexation and lethargy descending over me once again. I had incorporated special Christmas touches throughout the house. Taking it all down, organizing everything back into their bins, and storing them again in closets and under beds was a daunting task.

I opened the first closet to retrieve the empty bins I needed. Distress washed over me. I slammed the door shut. Countless bins filled with unused decorations stood in the way of the empty bins. Opening the door again, I stared at the mound of work ahead of me. In a flash, my thoughts turned to the relaxing and memorable Christmas we had just shared minus all those unused trimmings. I made a command decision. All that extra stuff had to go. Energized, I gathered the mountain of bins, Christmas trees, and boxes and carried them straight to my van. I promptly delivered it all to our church for the upcoming yard sale. As I put down the last box, delight coursed through me like a gulp of iced tea on a hot summer day. Back at the house, with my vigor renewed, I took down and stored our decorations in record time.

The final dreaded job on my checklist remained beyond our bedroom door. Mayhem. There was no better word to describe our usually serene room. It had become the dumping ground for excess furnishings and items to allow more space for our visitors. Remnants of Amazon delivery boxes along with rolls and rolls of wrapping paper covered most of the floor. The corners were filled with who-knew-what, and you couldn't see the loveseat for the pile of laundry. Every flat surface was crowded with items that belonged elsewhere. The room that usually offered me respite now seemed to close in on me.

The condition of the room overwhelmed me, but it had been more than that. Something else about this room disabled me. Gazing around, I made the revealing connection. The room mirrored my turbulent spirit which was also cluttered with too much that didn't belong. The room was a mess and so was I. Realization dawned. Downsizing the glut of decorations and having the rest of the house back to normal had not completely alleviated the turmoil in my spirit. I whispered, "What do You want me to do, Lord?" The flow of grace led to understanding. God had been prodding me to let go of not only excess stuff in my home, but also a number of taxing responsibilities. Then and there I resolved to delegate many of my duties to other members of the women's retreat team. It was also time for the men's team to handle all of their administrative tasks. Immediate peace flooded my spirit. I practically floated from the magnitude of the release. Full of joy, I restored our poor burdened room to the sanctuary it was meant to be.

My Heavenly Father knew I needed to let go of many things. I had been overextending myself. The clutter in my life was blocking the flow of the Holy Spirit. God invited me into this new season of letting go where I was free to take hold of His hand and accompany Him along the path He had prepared for me.

Annette Wiley's writing odyssey began as daily journaling. The twists and turns of twenty-one years as a military wife provided plenty of material for her musings. She often speaks with various women's groups, sharing her enlightening reflections. Annette resides in South Carolina with Larry, her husband of forty-six years.

*Southern California
Christian Writers' Conference*

You Are Loved

Kim Caroline

Heavenly Father,
We praise You for Your holy, beautiful presence
with our lives and in our world.
We put on the righteousness of Your Son
remembering His sacrifice and passion for us.
We take on His beauty, loving-kindness, and grace today.
Thank You for Your promise
that You are with us always.
When we were Your enemies because of our sin
You still loved us.
When we pass through rising waters
You are with us.
When we fail and disappoint,
living with our own regret and shame
You mercifully uplift us.
Thank You for Your comfort,
Your hope and Your belief in us.
When we have tried, failed, and given up,
when others have walked away,

when You are our last resort instead of our first,
Thank You for forgiveness.
Thank You for embracing us yet again with open arms
saying You'll never leave us or forsake us.
For forgiving us, loving us,
delighting in us, celebrating us…
There's none like You, Father
and You will never ever change.
We worship You
living, breathing, existing by Your hand alone,
trusting in Your glorious, infinite love,
swimming in Your mercies undeserved.
You alone are God.
Use my life for Your glory and kingdom
I love You and bless Your name today.

Amen.

Caroline Kim has been in prayer ministry for twelve years, including serving as an intercessory missionary at the International House of Prayer in Kansas City. She writes prayers daily for her blog thecreativepray.com, and currently lives with her family in Orange County, California.

How to View Your Life Like a Rubber Band

G. Yvonne Mallory

I had never thought much about rubber bands until one morning when I was meditating on Jesus being a gardener (John 15). As an experienced gardener, He knew how necessary it was to prune His garden to keep it healthy and strong. I thought about the word "pruning" for a long time. This process requires removing dead, broken, or damaged branches, cleaning to remove disease, cutting or shortening branches to train them so they don't go astray or hit other objects, and thinning to permit more sunlight to come through. Suddenly, the connection between rubber bands and pruning was remarkable.

Rubber bands are used for a variety of reasons. Sometimes I use them to keep things closed, and sometimes I use them to hold things together. But the process for making rubber bands consists of a variety of complicated actions. Starting with natural rubber slabs, the rubber band making business involves the use of water, talcum powder, certain chemicals, a mechanized rolling pin, an oven, extruding machine, and long tubes. When the process is finished, the rubber band is strong enough to withstand stretching and flexible enough to be used in a variety of ways.

When we are stretched, we become more flexible; when we are pruned, we become stronger and healthier, able to bear more fruit with every circumstance God allows.

When stressful situations enter our lives, uninvited, they can seem like a truck driving through the front door. We become anxious and want immediate resolution, or, at the very least, a quick change for the better. When certain people come into our space and sabotage our emotions, we sometimes become impatient and angry. A display of anger, impatience, or lack of self-control can destroy a relationship. A crucial point to keep in mind: *there **will always** be people and situations in our lives that require patience.* Patience does not mean to curl up in a cocoon and lose hope. If we murmur and complain, interestingly, the circumstances either do not change, or they become even more unpleasant.

Like a rubber band, unexpected challenges will stretch us, quite often for an extended period of months, or even years. It may mean changing your expectations and looking for the positive aspects of the experience that produce character building, expressions of thankfulness, and having faith/hope that God will bring the solution that creates the best plan for you (Romans 8:28).

Stretching builds our character and creates enduring trust in Him. During these rubber-band situations, trust that the creativity of God is always active. His stretching will require patience and endurance from you, which means standing firm despite the obstacles or pain (James 1:2-8). Job (pronounced *Jobe* with a long O), throughout several months of extreme pain and suffering, exhibited patience, endurance, and faith. The reward for his patience was monumental (Job 1-42). Athletes become great through their display of patience and endurance, and they do not quit every time they experience pain. Rubber bands are useful because they can be stretched, which makes them remarkably resilient for many purposes.

Have you ever wondered why a rubber band loses its elasticity (stretchiness)? I read that over time, the ingredients called "volatiles," which keep it soft and flexible, evaporate, and it becomes rigid and breaks. In the same way, people often become hardened and inflexible, like a stiff rubber band. This is more likely to happen when we lose our trust in God. We forget He has all the ingredients to shape and mold us so that we remain mature, strong, and purposeful.

To achieve the benefit from our stretching moments, it may mean a change in thinking. Discipline yourself to embrace change; be flexible and open to adjustment; seek the truth; look for better ways to accomplish certain daily things; practice being grateful.

We use rubber bands in many ways. We should view ourselves as being created to be used by God for His perfect mission for us. What better way for Him to accomplish His purpose than to stretch us like a rubber band beyond our comfort zone (James 1:3-4).

G. Yvonne Mallory (Yvonne) hosts a website *Emeth In Agape (Truth In Love)*, www.yvonnemallory.com featuring personally written articles called *Spiritual Nuggets, Words to Help You Leap Over the Bumps in Your Life Journey*. She provides audio insights for each life topic. Yvonne currently has a nonfiction book in progress.

Whispers of Grace

Most Powerful Force

D.H. Weinberg

Grace is the most powerful force on earth
Stronger than hate
Stronger than punishment
Stronger than even love
Because love doesn't require we mess up
Whereas with grace, we know
We are totally undeserving and unworthy of it

Grace rocks us to our very core
When we receive grace
We are helpless to understand "how and why"
Since we know inside we're wrong or guilty
Grace for us seems unjust, and makes no sense
Like it does to those to whom we give grace
To people who DON'T deserve it
To people who have hurt us deeply
And yet, we do it anyway
Following God's example

Grace is able to overcome the irreconcilable
Things that can never be forgotten, never made whole
Grace is able to melt the coldest, the hardest heart
And restore "impossible" relationships

And we don't possess it – only God has it
But He gives it away to those who ask Him
To all of us, saved by grace,
For us to freely share with others.

D.H. Weinberg is a new author who comes out of a career in the business world, and seeks to enlarge people's vision and hunger for God. He has created manuscripts across multiple genres including devotionals, suspense thrillers, and young adult historical fiction.

Gracie

Janene Zirges

My heart was pounding so loudly it drowned out the clamoring voices around me. Drowning. Forever will the thought haunt me. I must repress the desire to gasp for air, just as my little Gracie was a few hours before. How could I have missed it, not sensed that something was wrong? She was right next to me, playing with her cousins she met for the first time today. Usually Gracie was somewhat shy with first meetings, but not this time. Her older cousins scooped her up and doted on her all morning. When our cheerful conversations switched to lunch preparations, none of us noticed the kids had gone to the swings—all of them except for Gracie. How did she get through the closed gate to the pool? I should have been watching more closely. She had not even had her first swim lessons. That is the first thing...Oh, dear God! Please let our sweet Gracie live to see her first swim lessons. Lord, haven't we had enough sorrow and loss?

Gracie was our little miracle, our precious gift from God. The years of trying to have a child of our own were exhausting. No. Exhausting and gut wrenching. Two miscarriages, more false alarms than I care to count. We finally resolved that God had chosen to leave us childless, which seemed out of place since both of us came from large, close-knit families. With that realization I had two choices— turn my back on God and this cruel joke or embrace this reality and immerse myself in the balm of God's Word. I chose the latter, and ever so gently, the God of grace and comfort spoke to my broken, tormented heart. Psalms of comfort were my refuge, as in Psalm 119:50, *This is my comfort in my affliction, that your promise gives me life*, and Psalm 119:76, *Let your steadfast love comfort me according to your promise to your servant.* Over the next year and a half, I slowly began to find myself giving comfort rather than needing it. Women struggling with infertility seemed to gravitate toward me, and at first, I was a bit irritated by it. Did they not know some of my own wounds were still open? The announcement of another pregnant mama at church. Invitations to birthday parties of my nieces and nephews. I was excited for every announcement, and rejoiced with them, but my heart still ached for the chance to love and nurture a babe of my own. I continued to listen for God's reassurance, as well as direction for our future. My ever patient and compassionate husband held me when the burden was heavy, whispering words of comfort. For some, the heartache of infertility means a marriage of painful reminders and insurmountable hurdles; yet for David and me, we were drawn closer together by encouraging, praying, talking, and listening to each other every single day. By God's grace, I had emerged from this struggle scarred, but stronger…and I thought, ready for anything. Then one day a sweet young woman shared her testimony at a women's tea that struck me to my core. She shared her story of adoption and the impact her adoptive family had on her life. She trusted that God had directly placed her in the exact family she would need to thrive, to be accepted and loved unconditionally. She shared Psalm 68:5-6, *A father to the fatherless, a defender of widows, is God in his holy dwelling. God sets the lonely in families.* This verse resonated over and over in my head. God had been nudging me ever so gently, but now I felt as though he had given me a big push. God had carefully planted the seed that we could be a loving family for a lonely child who needed a place to call home. David and I had never really talked about adoption, so I hesitated to bring it up. Funny how God orchestrates things. We went out on a pizza date a few days later and had barely finished saying grace when David began to tell me about the interview he heard on the radio and wondered out loud if God might be calling us to adopt. Well I must have looked quite silly with my mouth gaping open, cheese and pizza sauce hanging from my speechless lips. We were both astonished, him by my reaction and me by his question. Yet, from that moment forward there was a barrage of emotions…tears, laughter, and making plans. We were going to adopt!

And adopt we did. A few months of paperwork, approvals, checklists, classes, more approvals, interviews, and yes, more checklists, but finally we were ready for the waiting. At least when one is pregnant, barring any complications, the timeline is pretty set. Not so with adoption. With that final approval, we were on God's timeline…two weeks, four months, a year. Oh, how I prayed it would not be months of waiting. It was all in God's hands. And though my heart still ached for a tiny babe, my head said be prepared for that energetic toddler or inquisitive preschooler.

One evening, after a long week, I sat with my legs up trying to imagine what it might be like with swollen ankles, backaches, and sleepless nights. Well…the sleepless nights I did not have to imagine. I often lay awake praying for the woman who would give my child life. Had she given up her sweet child years ago under trying circumstances? Or had she just found out she was pregnant, scared, and unprepared? As I whispered a prayer for her once again, I was startled by my phone vibrating on the table next to me. Who in the world would be calling me this late? Everything seemed to move in slow motion, but somehow, we were out the door in minutes. At the hospital there was a flurry of papers to sign and then more waiting as our little girl pushed her way into the world. And then it hit me. I choked back tears as I realized God was graciously giving us a newborn! What I longed and hoped for, God was bringing about. My heart was torn between those treasured memories and the reality of what we were facing here and now—then the uncontrollable sobs came.

In that moment of brokenness, the strong arms of David engulfed me, and my sobs relented into mournful tears. Oh God, I can remember how so completely fulfilled my heart was when sweet Gracie was placed into my eager arms just three short years ago. Please Father, let me hold her, and smother her with kisses and snuggles again. God be gracious to me today. Tell me loud and clear how you are going to make this heartache and pain disappear. Declare some prophetic word, to assure me you will fix this sorrow that threatens to overtake me.

Yet, in His wisdom God knew what I would need to survive this ordeal, no matter what the outcome. I would need His still small voice to drown out the fear and anguish that was shouting doubts in my ears. He knew I would need his whispers of grace as I blamed myself that our sweet Gracie was fighting for her life. Over the din of the beeping of monitors, the tears of concerned family and friends, and a million questions, I had become paralyzed, numb, wanting only to hear my Abba Father whisper in my ear and tell me Gracie would overcome yet another obstacle in her short little life.

Please, dear God! Show us your grace, show *me* your grace! After all, isn't that why we named her Gracie Hope? For in your mercy and grace, you saw fit to give us hope when we were hopeless, in giving us the most beautiful child we really did not deserve, but with whom we are so incredibly blessed. Give us more time, Lord.

David lifted my chin, looking into my pleading eyes. "The doctor says we can go sit with Gracie." Oh, Lord, I want to run to her, but I am exhausted. My feet feel like bags of sand. Father God give me strength to not fall apart when I see her. As I turn the corner into her room, I am amazed at how serene and calm she looks.

"Sweet Gracie, Mama loves you so much. Daddy, too. I am so sorry I wasn't there for you. But we are here now, and I am just going to sit here and hold your hand until you wake up."

The minutes melted into hours, but I remained vigilant in prayer and in my pleas for God's unmerited favor. As exhaustion overcame me, I had to wipe away the steady flow of tears. I feared the worst was inevitable. My heart was breaking. And then as if God were whispering his grace to me once again, I hear this raspy little voice whisper to me ever so gently, "It's okay, Mama. God said I could stay with you."

And my heart was full, once again.

Janine Zirges loves God and lives in Garden Grove, California, with her husband Phil of thirty-four years. They have four grown children and five adorable grandchildren. She loves words and loves to tell a story. Her current project is nonfiction. She also writes poetry, short stories, fiction or nonfiction, and devotions.

Living Parables of Central Florida, Inc., of which EABooks Publishing is a division, supports Christian charities providing for the needs of their communities and are encouraged to join hands and hearts with like-minded charities to better meet unmet needs in their communities. Annually the Board of Directors chooses the recipients of seed money to facilitate the beginning stages of these charitable activities.

Mission Statement

To empower start up, nonprofit organizations financially, spiritually, and with sound business knowledge to participate successfully as a responsible 501(c)3 organization that contributes to the Kingdom work of God.

GPS Grant Program

GPS–Godly Positioning System—helps charities and non-profits position themselves, through our business coaching and the supply of grant funding, so they can succeed long-term in fulfilling their callings to minister to the unmet needs in their communities.

www.ingramcontent.com/pod-product-compliance
Lightning Source LLC
Chambersburg PA
CBHW072014060426
42446CB00043B/2547